Anon(ymous)

A DRAMA BY

Naomi Iizuka

BASED ON HOMER'S *ODYSSEY*

The Rules in Brief

- DO NOT perform this Play without obtaining prior permission from Playscripts, and without paying the required royalty.

- DO NOT photocopy, scan, or otherwise duplicate any part of this book.

- DO NOT alter the text of the Play, change a character's gender, delete any dialogue, cut any music, or alter any objectionable language, unless explicitly authorized by Playscripts.

- DO provide the required credit to the author(s) and the required attribution to Playscripts in all programs and promotional literature associated with any performance of this Play.

Copyright Basics

This Play is protected by United States and international copyright law. These laws ensure that authors are rewarded for creating new and vital dramatic work, and protect them against theft and abuse of their work.

A play is a piece of property, fully owned by the author, just like a house or car. You must obtain permission to use this property, and must pay a royalty fee for the privilege—whether or not you charge an admission fee. Playscripts collects these required payments on behalf of the author.

Anyone who violates an author's copyright is liable as a copyright infringer under United States and international law. Playscripts and the author are entitled to institute legal action for any such infringement, which can subject the infringer to actual damages, statutory damages, and attorneys' fees. A court may impose statutory damages of up to $150,000 for willful copyright infringements. U.S. copyright law also provides for possible criminal sanctions. Visit the website of the U.S. Copyright Office (www.copyright.gov) for more information.

THE BOTTOM LINE: If you break copyright law, you are robbing a playwright and opening yourself to expensive legal action. Follow the rules, and when in doubt, ask us.

Cast of Characters

ANON

NEMASANI

NAJA

ALI

RITU

NASREEN

CALISTA

MR. YURI MACKUS

SEWING LADIES

SENATOR LAIUS

HELEN LAIUS

PASCAL

MR. ZYCLO

ZYCLO'S PET BIRD

BELEN

STRYGAL

NICE AMERICAN MOTHER

NICE AMERICAN FATHER

NICE AMERICAN DAUGHTER

SERZA

BARFLIES

IGNACIO

CHORUS OF REFUGEES

ENSEMBLE

Acknowledgments

Anon(ymous) was originally commissioned and produced in April 2006 by The Children's Theatre Company in Minneapolis, Minnesota. The cast and staff was as follows:

NEMASANI . . . . Rosanne Ma
ANON . . . . Michael Escamilla
MR. YURI MACKUS / STRYGAL /
LONE BARFLY / ENSEMBLE . . . . Terry Hempleman
SENATOR LAIUS / MR. ZYCLO /
NICE AMERICAN FATHER /
ENSEMBLE . . . . Steve Hendrickson
HELEN LAIUS / ZYCLO'S PET BIRD /
NICE AMERICAN MOTHER /
ENSEMBLE . . . . Annie Enneking
CALISTA / SEWING LADY #3 /
NICE AMERICAN DAUGHTER /
ENSEMBLE . . . . Becka M. Ollmann
NAJA / ENSEMBLE . . . . Sonja Parks
PROTEUS / ALI / IGNACIO /
ENSEMBLE . . . . Emil Herrera
NASREEN / SEWING LADY #2 /
BELEN / ENSEMBLE . . . . Hadija Steen-Omari
RITU / SEWING LADY #1 /
SERZA / ENSEMBLE . . . . Marvette Knight
PASCAL / ENSEMBLE . . . . Gavin Lawrence

Scenic Design . . . . Kate Edmunds
Costume Design . . . . Christal Weatherly
Lighting Design . . . . Geoff Korf
Music & Sound Design . . . . Andre Pluess, Ben Sussmann
Dramaturg . . . . Elissa Adams
Video Design . . . . Rebecca Fuller
Fight Choreography . . . . Edward "Ted" Sharon
Stage Manager . . . . Jenny R. Friend
Assistant Stage Manager . . . . Danae Schniepp
Apprentice . . . . Megan Traina
Dialect Coach . . . . Elisa Carlson

All production groups performing this play are required to include the following credits on the title page of every program:

> *Anon(ymous)* was originally commissioned and produced by The Children's Theatre Company of Minneapolis, Minnesota.

Michael Ray Escamilla and Sonja Parks in the World Premiere of *Anon(ymous)*, Children's Theater Company, Minneapolis (2006). Photo: Rob Levine.

ANON(YMOUS)
by Naomi Iizuka

1.

(Light on ANON.*)*

ANON. Where I come from is far away from here.

(CHORUS OF REFUGEES *emerges from the darkness.*)

CHORUS OF REFUGEES.
Where I come from is oxen in rice fields
and hills the color of green tea.

Where I come from is jungles filled with jaguars
and pythons thick as a grown man's thigh.

Where I come from is poison frogs the size of a thumbnail and squirrels that can fly from tree to tree.

Where I come from is waterfalls taller than the tallest skyscraper

Is olive trees and ancient desert

Is sampans and temple bells

Is sandstorms

Is monsoon rains

Is tapir and okapi and electric blue butterflies with wings as wide as
my arms.

Where I come from is the smell of orchid and mango and ripe papaya

Is the smell of my mother's fried bread

Is the smell of yerba mate

Lemongrass

Horchata

Coconut milk

Pho

Fried squid

Cow's blood

Joss stick

Sheep's milk, fresh and warm.

(The sounds of war begin, faint and distant.)

CHORUS OF REFUGEES. Where I come from is high up in the mountains and the sound of thunder is so loud it sounds like the end of the world.

Where I come from is the edge of an ocean so blue you can see straight to the bottom, and the sound of the waves crashing is so loud it sounds like the end of the world.

Where I come from giant birds circle overhead, so many you can't count them all, they caw caw caw, and the sound they make is so loud, it sounds like the end of the world.

(The CHORUS OF REFUGEES *disperses in all different directions.* NAJA *remains. The sounds of war grow closer.)*

NAJA. Do you remember?

ANON. No—

NAJA. All those memories—

ANON. I don't remember—

NAJA. Can you hear them—

ANON. No—

NAJA. You can't hear them, all those memories inside of you? You've locked them inside for so long and now they're pounding against your rib cage, against the walls of your heart. Can you hear them? Listen.

(Whispered fragments from the first chorus. The sounds of war grow closer.)

ANON. I don't know how to begin. I don't know where to begin.

NAJA. Sssssssh.
Begin in the middle.
On the border.
On the crossing.
Begin in the place in between.

(NAJA begins to recede from view. Night falls. The sky is vast and inky blue. The sounds of war grow closer. Distant gunfire. The whistling of bombs falling from the sky.)

2.

(ANON *is alone in the night.*)

ANON.
Where I come from is far away from here.
Where I come from there was a war that lasted so long
People forgot what they were fighting for.
Where I come from bombs rained down from the sky night after
  night
And boys wandered the streets with M-16s.
Where I come from mines are planted in the roads like deadly flowers,
And the air smells like death, rank and sticky sweet.
Where I come from you go to sleep at night
And dream about the faces of the people you love.

(*Light on* NEMASANI. *She sings an ancient song.* ANON *sees
her.*)

ANON. You dream the face of the one person you love. And that
person, that person becomes like home. Their eyes. Their skin. Their
voice, the sound of their voice. And so you dream about that person.
You dream about home. You dream about going home.

(ANON *approaches* NEMASANI. *The sounds of war grow.
They get so loud. It sounds like the end of the world. The whistling
sound of a bomb falling from the sky. The whistling grows louder,
closer.* NAJA *emerges from the darkness. She pulls* ANON *out of
the path of the bomb. They leap into a vast, uncharted darkness.
An explosion, blinding white light. The sounds of war transform
into the sound of sewing machines.*)

3.

(*A sewing factory in a city somewhere in America. The sound of
the sewing machines like a hive of metallic bumblebees. A mountain of fabric reaching up to the heavens. Rows of sewing machines
one after the next as far as the eye can see. The* CHORUS OF
SEWING LADIES *sews in perfect unison.* NEMASANI *is one
of the sewing ladies. She sews a shroud. Enter* MR. YURI MACK-
US, *the manager of the sewing factory. He escorts* SENATOR *and*
MRS. LAIUS *around the factory floor.*)

MR. MACKUS. *(To* SENATOR LAIUS:*)* The first thing I want to say is we are not a sweat shop. We are the first stop on the way to the American Dream. Give us your poor, your huddled masses yearning to be free and we'll hire them, we'll give them a job, we'll put them to work, nothing wrong with good honest work. As you can see, Senator, the conditions here are first-rate. Light and airy. Modern. Cheerful. We have a great time—don't we, ladies? All the ladies love me and I love them.

SENATOR LAIUS. *(To the* SEWING LADIES:*)* Don't mind us please don't mind us. We're just here to observe.

MRS. LAIUS. *(To the* SEWING LADIES:*)* What are you making?

CHORUS OF SEWING LADIES.
Blue jeans
T-shirts
Yoga pants
Sports bras.

Boxer shorts
Warm up jackets
Polo shirts
Tube socks.

Short shorts
Sweatshirts
Khaki pants
Baseball caps.

Mini-skirts
Baby bonnets
Oxford shirts
Bikini tops.

MRS. LAIUS. *(Seeing* NEMASANI's *shroud:)* Oooooh I love this. What is it?

NEMASANI. A shroud.

MRS. LAIUS. Oooooh a shroud. How interesting. What's a shroud?

NEMASANI. It's a sheet you wrap around the dead.

MRS. LAIUS. Oh. Oh I see. And do you sell a lot of those? Shrouds, I mean.

NEMASANI. It's not for sale.

MRS. LAIUS. It's lovely, the design is just lovely. I collect primitive art, you know, from all around the world. It's a passion of mine. I have baskets from Guatemala and little buddhas from Cambodia. They speak to me. This speaks to me. I would love to buy this and hang it on my wall.

NEMASANI. It's not for sale.

MR. MACKUS. Don't mind Penny.

NEMASANI. My name's not Penny.

MR. MACKUS. Her real name is too hard to pronounce. We call her Penny. It's easier. Isn't it, Penny?

SEWING LADY #1. Mr. Mackus wants to marry Penny. He proposes to her everyday. "Will you marry me, Penny," he whispers in her ear. He gets so close she can smell his breath. Coffee and Tic Tacs. She tells him she'll say yes when she finishes the shroud.

MR. MACKUS. I love Penny. I want to give her a good home. She's had a very hard life. I'm just doing my part. I have a big heart. It's my undoing.

SEWING LADY #1. Mr. Mackus had a mail order bride from Russia.

MR. MACKUS. Not true —

SEWING LADY #1. And one from the Philippines —

MR. MACKUS. Lies lies all lies —

SEWING LADY #1. And one from Thailand, Romania, and Honduras —

MR. MACKUS. THAT'S ENOUGH!

MRS. LAIUS. Who's it for? The shroud, I mean.

NEMASANI. My son.

MRS. LAIUS. Your son? Is he dead? That's so sad. That makes me very, very sad.

SENATOR LAIUS. Helen, darling —

MRS. LAIUS. You must be devastated. You poor thing. How did he die?

NEMASANI. He drowned.

MRS. LAIUS. He drowned! That's awful. It's so tragic, it's just so tragic. I feel your pain, I really do. How did it happen? If you don't mind me asking. It helps sometimes to talk, you know, to share. That's what human beings do, they share, they share their joy, they share their pain, it's only human, we're only human, you can tell me, go on tell me — and maybe I can help.

(The sewing factory transforms into the ocean.)

4.

(Night. The ocean. Light on ANON. He holds a toy boat which he steers through a dark ocean. It's night.)

NEMASANI. Where we come from, there was a war. And my son and me, we escaped. We escaped in the middle of the night. We sailed out to sea in an old fishing boat. There were so many people all crammed together, old people and little babies. We huddled together in the dark in the belly of the ship. We listened to the roar of the waves. We listened to the boat creak and moan. And then the storm started.

(The storm begins. Lightning. Thunder.)

NEMASANI. The winds began to howl. The sky opened up and the rain came down, sheets and sheets of rain. And the lightning lit up the sky, bright bright light, and the thunder crashed. And the sound was so loud. And suddenly a giant wave rose up. It rose and it rose like a wall of water, and then it fell over us, and swallowed us whole.

(The wave crashes down. Darkness.)

5.

(The sound of the surf. Light up on a tropical beach somewhere in America. A boy named ANON and a girl named CALISTA sit on the beach. CALISTA wears a bathing suit. ANON wears street clothes. ANON examines the broken toy boat. CALISTA has a camera. She takes pictures. Music plays on a portable CD player.)

ANON. Someday I'm going to sail away.

CALISTA. No you're not. Don't be silly. You're not going anywhere. This is your home now.

ANON. It's not my home.

CALISTA. Yes it is.

ANON. It's not my real home.

CALISTA. Yes, it is. Now look at me. Look at me. Smile. I SAID SMILE.

(CALISTA snaps a photo of ANON.)

CALISTA. You're very photogenic. You could be a male model. You're so swarthy and exotic. That's very in right now. Exotic is very in. I wish I were more exotic. I'm too pale. I wish I had a tan. I wish my skin was the color of café au lait.

(A new song begins on the portable CD player.)

CALISTA. Oooooh I love this song.

(CALISTA dances. and then she stops.)

Do you want to watch TV. We could watch TV on my giant flat screen plasma TV. It's so cool. It's so flat.

ANON. No thanks.

CALISTA. What about a snack?

(CALISTA retrieves a bag of candies. She begins to eat. She eats a lot. She stuffs her face with candy.)

CALISTA. I have M&Ms and Kit Kats and Nestlé's Crunch and Snickers and Reese's Pieces and Charleston Chews and Sweet Tarts and Lemon Heads and Skittles and Spree.

ANON. I'm not hungry.

CALISTA. Suit yourself.

CALISTA. We could do something else. We could kiss. You could kiss me. Do you want to kiss me?

ANON. No.

CALISTA. That's OK. You can kiss me later.

ANON. I'm never going to kiss you.

CALISTA. Fine.

ANON. Not now or later. Not ever.

CALISTA. FINE! *(Pause.)* Why are you so mean to me? You should be nice to me. I saved your life. You washed up on the shore of my dad's luxury beachfront condo and you weren't even breathing. I fished seaweed out of your mouth. I administered C.P.R. I gave you the kiss of life just like I learned in summer camp. And I thought you were so handsome and exotic and not like any of the boys from around here. I saved your life and you're so ungrateful! You won't even tell me your real name!

ANON. I told you my real name.

CALISTA. Your real name is not "Nobody." What kind of mom names their kid "Nobody"?

ANON. Don't talk about my mom.

CALISTA. I mean I'm sure she was nice and all, but it's not even like she's even part of your life anymore. I mean she's probably dead and even if she's alive, it's not like she's been trying that hard to find you. Honestly, if you want my opinion, she's probably moved on with her life. I know I would. I bet if you showed up on her doorstep like right this second, she probably wouldn't even know who you were. She'd probably be like: "Who are you? Do I know you?"

ANON. I SAID DON'T TALK ABOUT MY MOM! *(Pause.)* OK look, I can't stay here anymore. I can't do it.

CALISTA. Why not? It's nice here. It's pretty and clean. And I have satellite TV.

ANON. I gotta go. I'm going to lose my mind if I have to stay here one more day.

CALISTA. Where would you go?

ANON. Home.

CALISTA. But this is your home.

ANON. My real home.

CALISTA. Your "real home"? That's crazy. Your "real home" is a dirty little third world shack with no running water. It's raw sewage in the streets and malaria and cholera and all kinds of disgusting parasites I don't even want to think about. I'm just saying how it is. Don't be mad. Now you're mad. Let's kiss and make up.

ANON. No.

CALISTA. Why not?

ANON. Because I hate you and every time you open your mouth, I want to stuff sand down your throat.

CALISTA. OK you know what? I don't care. I don't care what you think. I don't care what you want. You will eat my Skittles and my Kit Kats and my Spree. You will enjoy my flat screen plasma TV. And you will love me.

(Enter NAJA *from the ocean. She's a surfer. She wears a wetsuit. She has a surfboard.)*

NAJA. Hey.

ANON. Hey.

NAJA. Remember me?

ANON. Yeah. Kinda.

CALISTA. Where did you come from?

NAJA. He called me.

ANON. I did?

NAJA. He sent telepathic brain waves out into the universe and I was listening.

ANON. You were?

NAJA. I was. I'm a really, really good listener.

ANON. That's cool.

NAJA. I know.

ANON. That's really cool.

NAJA. I know.

CALISTA. Uh, excuse me. Who are you?

NAJA. I'm a goddess. And you are?

CALISTA. I live here. My dad owns this place. He owns everything as far as the eye can see. He's very, very powerful. That's who I am.

NAJA. Is that supposed to impress me?

CALISTA. I'm just saying how it is.

NAJA. You know? You're like really pale.

CALISTA. Yeah? Well you're like really rude.

NAJA. Yeah, but you're really pale. How does a person get to be so pale? You're like Wonder Bread. You're like mayonnaise.

CALISTA. I am not like mayonnaise. Cow.

NAJA. Hag.

CALISTA. Witch.

(NAJA *pulls* CALISTA's *hair.*)

CALISTA. OW! This is a private beach. So you better just take your stupid surfboard and take a hike.

NAJA. You can't own a beach.

CALISTA. Yes you can. My dad does. My dad owns the beach and the whole entire ocean.

NAJA. That's the stupidest thing I've ever heard. That's like saying you own a jungle or a mountain range.

CALISTA. My dad owns some of those, too. My dad is very rich.

NAJA. Yeah? Well if he's so rich, maybe he can buy you a better bathing suit because that bathing suit is ugly.

CALISTA. Shut up.

NAJA. It's like the ugliest bathing suit I've ever seen.

CALISTA. Shut up!

NAJA. *(To* ANON:*)* So you want to go or what?

ANON. Like now?

NAJA. Like right now, Like right this second.

CALISTA. He's not going anywhere. He's not allowed.

NAJA. He's "not allowed"? Who says?

CALISTA. My dad. My dad says we have to stay inside our luxury gated community. My dad says it's dangerous out there. My dad says all these foreigners are flooding in with all their strange customs and their weird food, and they don't speak English, and they're not like us, and most of them are illegal, they're illegal aliens, that's what my dad says. Whenever he says that, I think of little green men in space suits, but that's not the kind of alien he means, it's different a kind of alien.

NAJA. You're an idiot.

CALISTA. Shut up.

NAJA. And your dad's an even bigger idiot.

CALISTA. My dad is not an idiot. My dad is really, really rich and really, really powerful. And you don't want to make him mad.

NAJA. Look, I don't care about your dad. I don't care what he thinks or says or does. I don't listen to people like your dad. And he doesn't either. *(To ANON:)* Right?

ANON. Right.

NAJA. Ready?

ANON. Yeah.

CALISTA. Wait. You can't go.

ANON. Yeah, I can. Watch me.

(ANON *and* NAJA *dive into the ocean.*)

CALISTA. WAIT! STOP! COME BACK! I'M GOING TO CALL MY DAD! AND THEN YOU'RE GOING TO BE SORRY!

(CALISTA's *voice becomes a tiny echo fainter and fainter.* CALISTA *becomes a tiny figure on the shore, a speck too small to see.*)

6.

(*The middle of a giant ocean.* ANON *and* NAJA *are floating. It's very calm.*)

ANON. The last time I was in the ocean, I almost drowned.

NAJA. I know.

ANON. I was with my mom. We were in an old fishing boat. We were trying to escape and there was a storm —

NAJA. I know.

ANON. How could you know that?

NAJA. You don't remember me do you?

ANON. Yeah I do. We knew each other when we were kids.

NAJA. Oh yeah?

ANON. Yeah. You lived across the street.

NAJA. Is that right?

ANON. Yeah. You lived in a big old building. It's not there anymore. The bombs fell and it was destroyed.

NAJA. I know. *(Pause.)* What was I like?

ANON. Kinda shy. Kinda cute. Your hair was different.

NAJA. Shorter? Longer?

ANON. Just different. I had a crush on you.

NAJA. Oh yeah?

ANON. Yeah.

NAJA. I think you're thinking of someone else.

ANON. Maybe. *(Pause.)* OK. I think I remember now. You were this girl at the airport.

NAJA. Yeah?

ANON. You were waiting to get on a plane. You were going somewhere far away. You were all by yourself. You were reading a book.

NAJA. What book?

ANON. It was a big book. I remember it was like this really big, old book. It was really, really big. The title is on the tip of my tongue.

NAJA. You don't remember me.

ANON. No, not really. But I feel like I do. I feel like I know you. I feel like I've known you my whole life.

NAJA. That's because I'm a goddess and I come to you in your dreams.

ANON. Really?

NAJA. Uh huh. And you're a mere mortal so you don't remember. Your brain's too small.

ANON. Is that how it works?

NAJA. Pretty much.

ANON. And what do you do? Like when you come to me in my dreams?

NAJA. I give you advice. I whisper it in your ear. Sometimes I save your life.

ANON. Is that right?

NAJA. Uh huh.

       (ANON *and* NAJA *kiss.*)

ANON. Do all goddesses kiss like that?

NAJA. No, just me.

(ANON *and* NAJA *kiss.*)

ANON. I'm really homesick.

NAJA. I know.

ANON. It's like a big empty room inside of me.

NAJA. I know.

ANON. What if you want to go home, but there's no more home to go home to? What if the one person you love more than anything, what if they don't remember you? What if they don't even know who you are?

NAJA. Sssssssh.

(NAJA *kisses* ANON. NAJA *pulls away.*)

NAJA. OK no more kissing. You have things to do.

ANON. Like what?

NAJA. Like survive the storm.

ANON. Why does there always have to be a storm? Why can't it just be smooth sailing?

NAJA. Don't ask why. Just start swimming.

(*The winds pick up. The clouds race. The sky darkens. The waves rise. A blinding light. A lightning flash. A clap of thunder.*)

ANON. WAIT!

(ANON *and* NAJA *are hurled in different directions.*)

7.

(*The ocean transforms into the sewing factory. The end of the day. The sewing factory is deserted. MRS. LAIUS and NEMASANI are alone. MRS. LAIUS has been listening to NEMASANI's story.*)

MRS. LAIUS. And your little boy? Did you ever see him again?

NEMASANI. No. Sometimes I think maybe he was saved. Maybe the Coast Guard found him. Or maybe he was able to swim to shore.

MRS. LAIUS. Wouldn't that be something.

NEMASANI. And then maybe he was adopted by a nice American family.

MRS. LAIUS. Yes! We adopted a little boy from the Third World. The senator and I found him in a refugee camp. He was so cute. We had such high hopes. But it didn't work out. He was nothing but problems from the start. He didn't blend in. He had a bad attitude. And then he ran away. Can you believe it? We gave him everything and he ran away.

NEMASANI. I think maybe my son, maybe he's alive somewhere.

MRS. LAIUS. Maybe. Probably not. But maybe.

(SENATOR LAIUS *and* MR. MACKUS *appear.*)

SENATOR LAIUS. Helen, darling, we really have to scoot.

MRS. LAIUS. I hope it all works out for you. I really do**SENATOR LAIUS.** Helen —

MRS. LAIUS. I mean I hope you can find closure and renewal. I find meditation and yoga, yoga can be really helpful, mindfulness and deep breathing —

SENATOR LAIUS. HELEN!

MRS. LAIUS. Coming, darling.

(MRS. LAIUS *and* SENATOR LAIUS *exit.* NEMASANI *returns to sewing the shroud.* MR. MACKUS *is holding bags of take-out.*)

MR. MACKUS. Mmmm. I ordered some take-out for the two of us. It's from this Indian place on the other side of town. I got us a little chicken tikka masala, a little papadum, a little naan. Mmmm. Taste.

NEMASANI. I'm not hungry.

MR. MACKUS. Marry me, you little vixen, you little minx.

NEMASANI. Mr. Mackus.

MR. MACKUS. You know you want to marry me. You find me irresistible.

NEMASANI. Mr. Mackus, please.

MR. MACKUS. This "playing hard to get," Penny, is getting really old. You either marry me or lose your job. I hate to be so blunt, but that's the way it is.

NEMASANI. Mr. Mackus, as I told you, in my homeland, it is customary —

MR. MACKUS. Yes yes yes, "it is customary to make a shroud in which to bury the dead."

NEMASANI. That is correct.

MR. MACKUS. Yes, but you're not dead. I'm not dead. We're alive, Penny. We're vital. We have needs and desires. We have appetites—

NEMASANI. Mr. Mackus—

(NEMASANI *smacks the advancing* MR. MACKUS.)

MR. MACKUS. OW!

NEMASANI. When I am done, we can get married.

MR. MACKUS. Can't you speed things up?

NEMASANI. It takes as long as it takes.

MR. MACKUS. What if I can't wait?

NEMASANI. Then you will incur the wrath of the gods. Bad luck like you have never seen before. Forget about the number 13. Forget about breaking a mirror or stepping on a crack. Do you want to tempt fate, Mr. Mackus? do you know what happens to mortals who tempt fate? Vultures pecking at your liver and your eyeballs for all eternity. Your arms and legs ripped from their sockets, your head pried loose from its neck. Your skull smashed against a rock, brain goo splattered all over the pavement—

MR. MACKUS. Fine. No need to agitate the gods. My little crab apple. My little peach pit. I'll wait. I can wait. Sweet dreams, my little sweet potato.

(*Exit* MR. MACKUS. *When* NEMASANI *is sure he is gone, she begins to undo the stitches of the shroud.* SEWING LADY #2 *peeks out from behind a sewing machine and sees what* NEMASANI *is doing.*)

8.

(*A police helicopter overhead. The chup chup chup sound of its propellers. A bright beam of light shines down. Night in a city somewhere in America. The sounds of a city at night. Freeway traffic. A constant twinkling stream of tiny cars. TVs and voices and the clanking of garbage cans and the beep beep beep of trucks backing up. Somewhere in the giant city, the sound of a song from somewhere far away.* NAJA *enters with a transistor radio from which the song is playing. She sets the radio down.*)

9.

(The song continues. An alley behind an Indian restaurant. A neon sign spelling "CURRY." NASREEN opens the back door with a bag of garbage. She tosses the garbage bag into the dumpster. She sees the radio. She approaches the radio. She sings along briefly to the song. NASREEN hears a sound coming from the dumpster. ANON appears from out of the trash in the dumpster. NASREEN grabs the radio to use as a weapon.)

ANON. I didn't mean to scare you.

NASREEN. You didn't scare me.

ANON. You look kinda scared.

NASREEN. Well I'm not.

ANON. Are you sure?

NASREEN. Yes.

ANON. You shouldn't be hanging out in dark alleys in the middle of the night. It's dangerous.

NASREEN. I don't care. I'm strong.

ANON. You don't look that strong.

NASREEN. Well I am.

ANON. It's OK. I mean you'd be OK no matter what. I'd protect you.

NASREEN. I don't need protecting.

ANON. Right, cause you're strong.

NASREEN. That's right. I am.

ANON. I believe you.

NASREEN. Good.

(Pause. The song on the radio plays.)

ANON. You have a nice voice.

NASREEN. No I don't.

RITU. *(Off:)* NASREEN!

ANON. I like that song you were singing.

NASREEN. It's old. It's the kinda stuff my mom listens to. My mom has a nice voice. She sings. I don't sing.

RITU. *(Off:)* NASREEN!

NASREEN. What's your name?

ANON. *(Seeing the "CURRY" sign:)* Koo ri.

NASREEN. I never heard that name before. What does it mean?

ANON. Quick-thinking.

NASREEN. Is it stinky in there?

ANON. Kinda. But the food's pretty good.

NASREEN. What food?

> (ANON *lifts up a to-go carton from the dumpster.*)

That's not food. That's garbage.

ANON. What makes it garbage?

NASREEN. It's in the garbage can.

ANON. Yeah but it's the same food. It's just in a different setting.

NASREEN. Sometimes, the customers order all this food and then they take just one bite, and they say it's too spicy, and so they send it back, and then we have to throw it away.

ANON. I like spicy.

NASREEN. Me, too. The hotter the better.

RITU. *(Off:)* NASREEN!

ALI. *(Off:)* Nasreen, what are you up to? Your mother has been calling and calling.

> (Enter ALI. *He is blind. He makes his way over to* ANON.)

ALI. Are you conversing with the cockroaches? What do the cockroaches have to say for themselves this evening? Perhaps they say: "Hello, Nasreen. How are you? Did you bring me some leftover curry or a few morsels of naan?"

> (ALI *is very close to* ANON. *He stops. He sniffs.*)

ALI. You're very pungent, Mister Cockroach. I smell a whiff of our delicious aloo gobi from last week. And there, there is our delectable chicken korma from just yesterday. And right there is our mouthwatering lamb saag. I have an excellent sense of smell. Do you speak?

ANON. Yeah.

ALI. Remarkable. A very large cockroach endowed with the gift of speech.

ANON. I'm not a cockroach.

ALI. Good, that's good. My wife kills cockroaches, you know. She crushes them with her shoe.

NASREEN. His name is Koo ri.

ALI. Koo ri?

ANON. Look I should probably go—

ALI. I'm Ali.

ANON. Nice to meet you, Mr. Ali, but—

ALI. Not Mr. Ali, just Ali. And this is my lovely daughter Nasreen. You've already met. I am the proprietor of this establishment. My wife Ritu is the chef. Each dish she makes is a masterpiece. The scents, the tastes of home in each delicious bite.

ANON. Look I really gotta go—

ALI. You will be our guest.

ANON. That's really nice of you, but I can't. I really have to get going—

ALI. I insist. I assure you it's more comfortable indoors. This way, please—

ANON. No see I can't do that. I can't stay -

ALI. Nonsense. Nasreen, set a table for our guest. Ritu, we have company!

(ALI *ushers* ANON *inside.* NASREEN *follows.*)

10.

(*The kitchen of an Indian restaurant. Steam and the sound of running water. Dishes piled high. The sound of chopping and the clattering of silverware and china. The hiss of the fry pan. A gust of flame. RITU is cooking. ALI and NASREEN sit at a table full of assorted hot peppers. ANON watches them from the edge of the room. ALI pops a pepper in his mouth.*)

ALI. It's so hot. It's hot hot hot. It's so hot I want to cry.

RITU. Ali, you're going to give yourself a belly ache.

ALI. Nonsense. I can take it.

(ALI *pops another pepper in his mouth.*)

RITU. Ali, stop. you're going to keel over.

ALI. (*Gasping:*) It's the pepper. It makes me sweat. It's very healthy.

RITU. You're turning red like a beet. Tell me this is healthy.

ALI. (*Picking up a tiny pepper:*) Very healthy.

NASREEN. It's so little.

ALI. Don't be fooled. It's the hottest pepper of them all.

RITU. Enough is enough. You eat that pepper, your tongue will fall out of your mulish old head.

NASREEN. What about our guest, poppa? Maybe he wants to try.

ANON. No, that's OK.

NASREEN. I thought you said you like spicy.

ANON. I do.

(NASREEN *takes the pepper from* ALI *and offers it to* ANON.)

NASREEN. Well here you go.

ALI. Nasreen—

NASREEN. But he said he liked spicy. That's what he said. Isn't that what you said?

ALI. Nasreen, my dove, there's spicy, and then there's *spicy*. I think our guest is wise enough to know the difference.

NASREEN. I think he's scared.

ANON. I'm not scared. How bad can it be?

NASREEN. Bad.

ALI. A burning inferno.

NASREEN. The death star of peppers.

(ANON *pops the pepper in his mouth.*)

ALI. Well?

(ANON *opens his mouth. He's swallowed the pepper.*)

NASREEN. He did it.

ALI. Impressive, stranger. I'm impressed.

RITU. I used to have a goat that could eat anything. Tin cans. Hub-caps. Hot peppers.

NASREEN. You did? What happened to him?

RITU. I chopped him up and made goat stew.

ALI. Ritu.

RITU. Where do you come from, stranger?

ANON. I'm from all over.

RITU. And your family? Where are they?

ANON. I don't know. I'm not sure.

RITU. I see. And what was your name again? I don't think I caught it.

ANON. Nobody. I mean Koo ri. I mean, nobody. I mean, I mean koo ri.

RITU. Koo ri or Nobody, which is it?

ANON. Nobody. I'm nobody.

RITU. Cooking for nobody, am I? That seems like a waste of perfectly good food.

ALI. Ritu, please.

RITU. You're too trusting, Ali. The city is full of liars and thieves. We don't know him. We don't know where he comes from. We don't know anything about him.

ANON. She's right. I should go. I'm really sorry —

ALI. No. You are our guest. Ritu has had a long day. Please forgive her.

RITU. Ritu has had many long days. Ritu has had many long weeks and months and years. And Ritu can speak for herself. (*To* ANON:) Here. I cooked it, you might as well eat it.

> (RITU *sets a plate of food down in front of* ANON. *She sets it down hard.*)

ANON. Thanks. Thank you.

> (ANON *eats in silence.* RITU *and* NASREEN *clean up.*)

ANON. Cumin, cinnamon, nutmeg, turmeric.
Allspice, cardamom, fennel, clove......coriander.

RITU. Yes, coriander. How did you know that?

ANON. My mom used the same spices. She just put them together differently.

NASREEN. Where is she now?

ANON. I don't know.

NASREEN. How can you not know where your mom is?

ANON. Where I come from, there was a war. There was a war and lots of people disappeared.

NASREEN. You mean they died.

RITU. Nasreen —

ANON. Some of them. But some of them, they just, they disappeared.

NASREEN. Maybe they escaped.

ANON. Maybe.

NASREEN. Maybe your mom escaped. Maybe she's living in the city somewhere and you just don't know it because she changed her name, but she's looking for you, too, only she doesn't know where to look because she came here from somewhere else, so she doesn't know how to get around. Lots of people come here from some place else. We did. Where we came from, there was a war, too.

RITU. Nasreen —

NASREEN. That's how my dad became blind. There was a bomb in the marketplace. Lots of people died, old people and little children —

RITU. Nasreen, that's enough. That was before. We don't talk about that now.

NASREEN. I don't remember where we came from. I was just a baby when we left.

ALI. You remember. You just don't remember that you remember.

NASREEN. How can I remember what I don't remember?

> (NAJA *enters. She's unseen and unheard by everyone except for* ANON.)

ALI. Sometimes in your dreams, something will bubble up from the depths, a tiny flicker of something you thought you forgot. A taste or a scent —

RITU. Jasmine.

ALI. Yes, jasmine.

> (NAJA *turns on the radio. An ancient song from far away.* ALI *caresses* RITU's *hair.)*

ALI. Your mother used to wear jasmine blossoms in her hair. I come across that scent sometimes and it takes me back. All of a sudden I think of something from years before, some tiny thing. A piece of a memory, like a shiny coin at the bottom of a well.

> (NASREEN *approaches* RITU *and* ALI. RITU *wraps her arms around her daughter.* ANON *watches the family from a distance.* NAJA *approaches* ANON.)

NAJA. What do you remember?

> (*The sounds of distant war.*)

ANON. I don't know where to begin. I don't know how. I don't know how to begin.

NAJA.
Begin in the middle
On the border
On the crossing.
Begin in the place in between.

> (*The sounds of distant war grow closer.* NAJA, ALI, RITU, *and* NASREEN *recede from view.*)

11.

> (ANON *remembers. Chaos in a burning city far away. The sound of rockets and mortars. Lightning. Thunder. The city transforms into an ocean. A tiny boat on a giant ocean. Night. He sees* NE-MASANI *She sings the same wordless melody she sang before.*)

ANON.
I remember my mom and how she used to hold me.
She held me when the bombs fell.
She held me when the ground shook and the city burned.
She held me on the night that we escaped.
She held me in the belly of the boat as we sailed across a giant sea.
I remember how she held me.
and then one night there was a terrible storm.

> (*A storm at sea. Winds howling. Sheets of rain. A terrible cracking sound. The boat splits apart. An explosion of water.* NEMASANI *vanishes under a giant wave.*)

12.

(The roar of the surf. ANON is in the ocean. Water as far as the eye can see. Night. Tiny lights shimmer in the distance.)

ANON. The next thing I remember: I was floating in a giant ocean. In the distance, I could see tiny lights. I started swimming towards them. I swam even though my clothes were soaked through and my arms and legs were numb, even though it hurt to breathe. I swam and I swam. I swam until I couldn't swim anymore. And then everything went black.

(Blackout. Everything is darkness.)

PASCAL. Pssst. Wake up. Wake up. Quick. Come on.

(The sound of a siren. Shouts. The sound of footsteps on pavement on steel containers. The clank of chainlink. The sound of running. ANON and PASCAL are running through the darkness. Glare of headlights. The sound of a city. They run. They run. They run.)

13.

(A tunnel underground. Graffiti and a giant L & N painted on the wall. The sound of rats. PASCAL and ANON catch their breath. PASCAL is West African. He has traditional scars on his face, thin horizontal lines.)

PASCAL. They won't come after us here.

ANON. Who were they?

PASCAL. Police. INS. Rent-a-cop. Who knows.

ANON. Where are we?

PASCAL. Tunnel.

ANON. What's that sound?

PASCAL. Rats. Giant rats. Five foot long, nose to tail. They live down here. They eat human flesh. They got a taste for it. They hunt for humans in the night. They go in packs. And if they find you alone and sleeping, they attack. They rip you to shreds. They tear out your insides. They rip out your still beating heart.

ANON. I didn't know rats came that big.

PASCAL. What? You don't believe me.

ANON. No.

PASCAL. Liar. You're scared. I can see it in your eyes.

ANON. I'm not scared.

PASCAL. Yeah you are. You ran like a little girl just now.

ANON. Then that makes two of us.

PASCAL. Come again?

ANON. I said that makes two of us. Little girl.

PASCAL. I'm not a little girl.

ANON. No you're right. You're just a liar.

PASCAL. What did you say to me?

ANON. You heard me. Liar.

> (PASCAL *rushes* ANON. *They fight. They fight. And then eventually they stop. A draw. They sit in the dirt in silence.*)

ANON. Why did you help me? Before, I mean.

PASCAL. I don't know. I guess you looked like you needed some help.

ANON. Thanks.

PASCAL. Whatever.

> (*They sit in silence.* PASCAL *pulls out potato chips from his bag.*)

PASCAL. Hungry?

ANON. Yeah.

> (PASCAL *shares his bag of potato chips with* ANON. *They eat.*)

PASCAL. Where did you learn English?

ANON. My mom, she taught me.

PASCAL. Yeah?

ANON. Yeah.

PASCAL. I'm Pascal.

ANON. (*Seeing the L & N sign:*) I'm Lan.

PASCAL. Lan, huh?

ANON. Yeah. Lan.

(PASCAL *and* ANON *stare each other down.* ANON's *eyes drift to the scars on* PASCAL's *face.*)

PASCAL. Didn't nobody tell you it's rude to stare.

ANON. Sorry.

PASCAL. Where I come from, they cut your face when you turn thirteen. Like a warrior. You got any scars?

ANON. No.

PASCAL. Everybody got scars. Maybe yours you just can't see.

(*A* SHADOW *emerges from the darkness looking for food.* ANON *starts for him.*)

PASCAL. (*Holding* ANON *back:*) Don't. He don't hurt no one. He lives down there.

ANON. What's wrong with him?

PASCAL. What's wrong with him? He's high. He's high as a kite.

ANON. He looks like someone I know.

PASCAL. Yeah? He could be. He won't remember if he is. His brain is fried. He don't remember nothing. He don't remember where he comes from, he don't remember his family, he don't remember the names of his kids. All he thinks about is getting high.

ANON. He must be lonely.

PASCAL. He ain't alone. He's got lots of company.

(*Other* SHADOWS *appear. They fill the tunnel. A faint rumbling.*)

Right on time. Come on, Lan. Or whatever your real name is.

(PASCAL *scrambles up a ladder to a ledge at the top of the tunnel. A bright light approaches.*)

You stay down there, you're gonna get squashed like a pancake. You think I'm foolin, you watch and see.

(*The rumbling gets louder. The light grows brighter.* ANON *hesitates, then scrambles up the ladder. The sound of steel against steel. The roar of a giant engine. A train bears down.* PASCAL *and* ANON *jump onto the roof of a boxcar. And then the train thunders past.*)

14.

(Night sky. Stars glitter. The top of the train speeding through the landscape. PASCAL and ANON on top of the box car.)

PASCAL. Listen.

(The sound of the train. A percussion of engines and metal. PAS-CAL taps out a beat. ANON joins him. Their rhythm builds. PASCAL stops tapping and looks at ANON. ANON notices that PASCAL is watching him and stops tapping.)

PASCAL. You know, you kinda look like a monkey.

ANON. I don't look like a monkey.

PASCAL. Yeah you do. Around the chin. And the ears. You have monkey ears. What's wrong with monkeys?

ANON. I don't look like a monkey.

PASCAL. Monkeys are good luck. Relax, monkey.

(The sound of the train. The landscape speeds by.)

ANON. How far does this go?

PASCAL. Far.

ANON. We could keep going and going.

PASCAL. We could, but we won't. We got a destination.

ANON. O yeah? Where's that?

PASCAL. A place I hear we can get some work, make a little money, get set up. Get some new clothes. You, monkey, are in need of new clothes.

ANON. What would you do if you had all the money in the world?

PASCAL. First, I'd buy a brand new car so I could go anywhere in style. Nice shiny rims, nice sound system so I could listen to my tunes. And then I'd eat all I could eat: steak and french fries and piz-za. I love pizza, pepperoni pizza. That's the best. What about you?

ANON. I don't know.

PASCAL. Yeah, you do.

ANON. I don't know. I guess I'd buy my mom a house, you know, a big house with a big yard so she'd never have to worry, so she'd always have a place where she could go. You know, a home.

PASCAL. A home, huh. That's nice. That's cool.

(*The sound of the train. The landscape speeds by.*)

PASCAL. Do you believe in fate?

ANON. Like fortune telling?

PASCAL. Kinda. Like everything that happens to you is already decided before you're even born.

ANON. And you don't have a choice?

PASCAL. No choice.

ANON. I don't know. I guess I don't think about stuff like that.

PASCAL. Where I come from, they try to tell your future from the stars.

ANON. Yeah? What do my stars say?

PASCAL. Hmmm. You will travel far. And have a bumpy ride.

ANON. You know what, I knew that already.

PASCAL. The stars don't lie.

ANON. No, they're just telling me what I already know.

PASCAL. Look at them all. So many stars. They look exactly like they do at home.

ANON. You think about home?

PASCAL. Not so much. How about you?

ANON. I think about my mom sometimes.

PASCAL. Yeah? What's she like?

ANON. I don't know how to describe her. Like a mom.

PASCAL. Does she smell like soap?

ANON. Yeah. Like soap and clean clothes and some kind of flower, I don't know what it is.

PASCAL. Does she have a big enormous bag she carries everything in?

ANON. Yeah.

PASCAL. Do her eyes crinkle up when she laughs?

ANON. Uh huh.

PASCAL. Does she sing sometimes when she thinks no one's listening?

ANON. Yeah.

PASCAL. Does she chop vegetables really fast?

ANON. So fast you can't even believe it. Yeah.

PASCAL. Does she sew?

ANON. Uh huh.

PASCAL. And when she sews, the stitches are so tiny and even, and you think how can they be so —

ANON. Perfect.

PASCAL. Yeah. I think about my mom, too.

ANON. Where's she now?

> *(The sound of the train begins to transform into a menacing rhythm of metal grinding against metal.)*

ANON. Pascal?

PASCAL. We're almost there.

ANON. Pascal?

> *(The sound of metal grinding against metal grows. It sounds like human voices wailing.)*

ANON. Pascal, where's your mom? Where is she now?

PASCAL. You know how to jump? You know how to fall? Watch. I'll show you.

> *(PASCAL jumps from the moving train. ANON follows.)*

15.

> *(ANON and PASCAL hit the ground. They tumble down a giant hill. The world is a blur. They tumble and roll, coming to a stop in front of a giant steel door. The door is ajar. The sound of opera. A ghostly fluorescent light from within. ANON and PASCAL enter. MR. ZYCLO sits alone in the room. He listens to opera on an old victrola. He is a butcher in a white coat with a tiny blood stain. He has one eye. He makes sausages with a meat grinder. He is surrounded by packages of frozen meat, raw and shrink-wrapped. ANON is transfixed by the packages of meat.)*

MR. ZYCLO. A good sausage is one of life's great pleasures. *(To PASCAL:)* Do you like sausage? Here. For you.

(PASCAL *approaches reluctantly, he eats the sausage.*)

MR. ZYCLO. You like that? My secret recipe. Top secret. *(To* ANON:*)* How about you? Sausage?

(ANON *doesn't move.*)

MR. ZYCLO. Don't you like sausage? No? No matter. More for me and your friend then.

(MR. ZYCLO *eats sausage ravenously.*)

PASCAL. We're looking for work.

MR. ZYCLO. What kind of work?

PASCAL. Whatever you have.

MR. ZYCLO. Times are tight. As you see, it's just me now. I had to let everyone else go.

PASCAL. We're good workers. We can do anything, anything you need.

ANON. Pssst. Pascal. Pascal—

PASCAL. What?

MR. ZYCLO. I could use some help cleaning up. I make a mess, my line of work.

PASCAL. We could do that. How much?

MR. ZYCLO. Trust me. I'll do right by you. What's the matter with your friend? Cat got his tongue?

ANON. What kind of meat is that?

MR. ZYCLO. Brain. It's a delicacy. High in protein. Very rich. Fry it up with a little garlic. Very tasty.

PASCAL. Where do we start?

MR. ZYCLO. There's a bucket and some sponges. I want you to scrub, scrub, scrub. I'll be back.

(MR. ZYCLO *exits. At the back of the room, there's another door.* ANON *examines the machine.* PASCAL *start to clean.* ANON *reaches out to touch the machine.*)

ANON. Look at this thing. Look at how sharp it is.

PASCAL. Leave it.

(ANON *moves away from the machine. He looks around the room.*)

ANON. It's cold.

PASCAL. Don't complain. We earn some money, and then we go.

ANON. How do we know he's gonna pay us?

PASCAL. He'll pay. Before you know it, we'll earn enough money, we can go anywhere. We can do whatever we want.

ANON. I don't like this place.

PASCAL. It's just a job. You think too much.

ANON. Maybe you don't think enough.

PASCAL. Maybe you should shut up.

> (ZYCLO'S PET BIRD *bursts through the door at the back of the room. She wears high heel shoes. She looks at* ANON *and* PAS-CAL. *She squawks and then exits. The click click click of her heels.*)

ANON. What's in there?

> (ANON *opens the door. Slabs of meat hang from hooks. Blood drips. The opera music grows in volume.* MR. ZYCLO *appears. He holds a hatchet. He approaches* PASCAL *and* ANON *as he speaks.*)

MR. ZYCLO. Have you seen my bird? I have a little pet bird. I feed her little morsels from my hand. She's very tame. I coo to her and she coos back. This is my freezer. It's very cold. Aren't you cold? I have to keep it cold like this or else the meat gets bad. Look at all this meat. Isn't it strange? When you cut off the head and scrape off the skin, when you boil away the fat and the gristle, it's hard to tell what something was. Was it a cow? Or a pig? Or a goat? Was it a little baby lamb? Or was it something else? A different kind of meat? Fleshy and tender and vaguely familiar. Do you know what goes into my sausages? Do you know what makes them so mouth-wateringly delicious? Do you have an idea? The tiniest inkling? What? Cat got your tongue?

> (MR. ZYCLO *raises the hatchet. Blackout. The sound of the hatchet whizzing through the air and then a dull thud as it hits. The sound of the giant steel door closing. The sound of opera stops. Then the sound of a bird whistling.*)

16.

(Lights up. The giant steel door to the outside is closed. MR. ZYC-
LO is making sausages with a meat grinder. Blood is everywhere,
on the floor, on the walls. His white coat is splattered with blood.
PASCAL is gone. ANON watches MR. ZYCLO. ZYCLO'S
PET BIRD clicks and paces frantically. The click click click of her
high heel shoes. She chirps and squawks and caws throughout the
scene trying to speak.)

ANON. Where's my friend?

MR. ZYCLO. What friend?

ANON. His name's Pascal. And he was here, he was right here just
a second ago.

MR. ZYCLO. There's nobody here named Pascal. You must be con-
fused. There's just me and you and my little pet bird.

ANON. He was right here. He was standing right here.

MR. ZYCLO. What was your name again? I don't think you ever said.

ANON. Uh, monkey.

MR. ZYCLO. Monkey. How delightful. You do look a little like a
monkey, one of those worried little monkeys you see in the zoo.
They look like little old men, nibbling on a piece of fruit, scratching
at their fleas, racing around their cage looking for a way out except,
of course, there is no way out.

(ZYCLO'S BIRD squawks.)

MR. ZYCLO. What a noisy bird. I used to have two, but then one of
them, he flew away.

(ANON tries to open the steel door.)

MR. ZYCLO. Now I keep the door shut tight or else she'll fly away,
too, and then I'll be all alone.

(ZYCLO'S BIRD squawks and caws frantically. A crescendo of
squawking.)

MR. ZYCLO. BE QUIET, BIRD, OR I'LL COOK YOU IN A POT. *(To*
ANON:) How do you like your meat, monkey? Well done or rare?

(ANON doesn't respond. MR. ZYCLO opens a box, takes out a
bottle of wine, uncorks it.)

MR. ZYCLO. "Rare, please. I like my meat rare." What about a glass of wine? "O yes please. A glass of wine would be delightful." Only, I have to tell you, I'm a little tired of cabernets. I prefer chianti. A good chianti can be just the thing.

(ZYCLO'S BIRD *chirps frantically to* ANON.)

ANON. I, I, I don't know much about wine.

MR. ZYCLO. No?

ANON. No.

MR. ZYCLO. Well why would you? It's just wine.

ANON. I've always wanted to learn.

MR. ZYCLO. Really.

ANON. I just never knew anyone who knew anything about wine. Not like yourself.

MR. ZYCLO. Some people are such snobs about wine. My feeling is, you like what you like. There's no right or wrong. There's only what you like. Here I'll show you.

(MR. ZYCLO *pours a little wine in a glass.*)

Now here we have a lovely vintage. Full bodied, robust. Twirl it, see how it streaks, That's what it should do, that's exactly what it should do. And then we sniff. And now we taste. Ah. Oaky.

(MR. ZYCLO *finishes the glass. And then he downs the bottle.*)

MR. ZYCLO. Fine wine is one of life's great pleasures. It's civilized. We live in nasty, brutish times. I try to remember what it is to be civilized. Linen napkins. Opera. Fine wine. Because it matters. It means something. But sometimes it can be so lonely, it can be so very lonely. You have no idea. It's nice to have someone to share a glass of wine with. I'll miss you when you go.

ANON. Go?

MR. ZYCLO. THWACK. THWACK. Sausage doesn't grow on trees. Sorry, monkey. That's just the way it is. And then it will just be me and my little bird. My little bird keeps me company, but she's sad. She had a little baby bird, but he flew away.

ANON. Maybe if you left the door open, he'd fly back.

MR. ZYCLO. O you're very tricky. But if I open the door, you'll run away, my little sausage-to-be.

ANON. Sssh. listen. I think I hear a bird outside.

(MR. ZYCLO *opens the heavy steel door.*)

MR. ZYCLO. No bird.

ANON. I swore I heard a bird just now.

(ZYCLO'S PET BIRD *chirps.*)

There. Listen.

(ZYCLO'S PET BIRD *chirps again.*)

MR. ZYCLO. Was that a bird? Cheep? Cheep? Cheep? O I feel so sleepy. So very very sleepy.

(MR. ZYCLO *collapses in a drunken stupor. ZYCLO'S PET BIRD comes over to ANON. The click click click of her high heel shoes. She takes her shoe off and gives it to ANON. ANON approaches MR. ZYCLO, raises the shoe and smashes it down. He puts out MR. ZYCLO's one good eye with the heel. MR. ZYCLO shrieks.*)

MR. ZYCLO. My eye! My eye! What have you done to my eye? I can't see. I can't see anything. My eye, my eye! It's killing me!

(MR. ZYCLO *hears ANON and his PET BIRD.*)

Little bird?

(MR. ZYCLO *approaches ANON.*)

Little bird? Is that you?

(MR. ZYCLO *lunges towards ANON. ANON overpowers MR. ZYCLO and shoves meat into his mouth.*)

ANON. HOW'S THAT? HOW DOES THAT TASTE? IS IT FULL-BODIED? IS IT ROBUST? IS IT CIVILIZED ENOUGH FOR YOU?

(MR. ZYCLO'S BIRD *shrieks. Frenzied, she descends on MR. ZYCLO. She is all nails and teeth and stiletto heels. MR. ZYCLO howls. A chaos of feathers and screeching and blood. ANON slips through the giant steel door.*)

17.

(ANON *runs. He runs. He runs. The world transforms into a giant freeway. The sound of the interstate like an ocean. Fields of tall grass as far as the eye can see. A wind makes the grass rustle and whisper.* ANON *doubles over, winded, unable to run any further.* IGNACIO *appears through the grass.*)

ANON. Hey. Wait. Which way do I go? I don't know which way to go. Say something. Why don't you say something?

(BELEN *appears behind* ANON. *She holds a small suitcase.*)

BELEN. He cannot.

(ANON *turns around, startled. He sees* BELEN. *The sound of the tall grass rustling and whispering.*)

My name is Belen. What's your name?

ANON. Nobody. I'm nobody. Do I know you? I feel like I know you.

BELEN. Maybe from a past life. Do you remember me from a past life?

ANON. I don't remember.

BELEN. When you die, they say you forget. You forget where you come from. You forget the people you love. That's what dying means: to forget. So you have to try very hard to remember. You have to keep what you love right in front of you, like a shiny coin at the bottom of a well.

(*The sound of* NEMASANI *singing.* NEMASANI *appears.* ANON *sees her.*)

ANON. I need to get back. I need to find my way back. I need to find my way home.

BELEN. Where's home?

ANON. Far away.

BELEN. How far?

ANON. Far. Very far.

(NEMASANI *fades away. The singing fades away. All that's left is the sound of the tall grass rustling and whispering.* IGNACIO *whispers to* BELEN.)

ANON. What's he saying?

BELEN. He says we should go now. He says we'll die if we stay here. He says if we're lucky a truck will come by and we can get a ride. He says I should go with you. He says you'll protect me. *(To IGNACIO:)* Poppa, wait —

> (BELEN *tries to follow* IGNACIO, *but she can't. He walks away into the tall grass without looking back. The wind murmurs. BELEN and* ANON *watch as* IGNACIO *disappears.)*

ANON. Why doesn't he come with us now?

BELEN. He would, if he could.

ANON. Why can't he?

BELEN. When my father left our village, he promised to come back and get me. He never made it. He died on his way back. Don't you see? My father is a ghost.

> *(The wind picks up. A howling wind. A truck thunders by. Headlights. The sound of brakes.)*

18.

> *(The cab of a truck speeding down the freeway.* STRYGAL *drives.* BELEN *sits between* ANON *and* STRYGAL. *The inside of the truck is hot. The faint sound of tapping.)*

STRYGAL. Hot enough for ya? Oooh boy is it hot. Never used to be this hot. It's the ozone. The ozone's all messed up. So where you kids headed to?

ANON. Home.

STRYGAL. Home sweet home. That's nice. So where's home? Far away is what I'm guessing. What's the matter? Cat got your tongue?

ANON. What did you say?

STRYGAL. What? Cat got your tongue? Ah it's just a thing my dad used to say.

ANON. Your dad? Who was your dad?

STRYGAL. Why do you care? He wasn't nobody. He was just a mean old drunk. Owned a butcher shop out in the boonies. Had one good eye. Can you believe it? Liked to listen to opera. If there's one thing I can't stand it's opera. I hate opera. *(To BELEN:)* Whaddya got in that suitcase, girly girl? Diamonds? Rubies? State secrets?

(STRYGAL *reaches over to touch* BELEN.)

ANON. Hey.

STRYGAL. Relax, pal. Relax. I was just picking some lint off the little lady's dress, just a little piece of fuzz. Hot, huh? It must be over a hundred. I'm sweatin like a pig.

(*The sound of tapping grows.*)

ANON. What's that sound?

STRYGAL. Could be the muffler.

ANON. What's in back? What are you hauling?

STRYGAL. This and that. It's a cash business. I don't ask a lot of questions.

ANON. I can hear something. There.

STRYGAL. Word to the wise, pal: keep your nose out of where it don't belong.

ANON. I think we should stop. I think we should stop and check.

STRYGAL. Look, I already stopped for you and your little friend here, out of the goodness of my heart. I'm not stopping anymore. I'm already running late. (*To* BELEN:) Anybody ever tell you, you're very pretty. You got very pretty hair.

(*The sound of tapping is joined by the distant sound of murmuring voices.*)

STRYGAL. This clown, he's not your boyfriend is he? He can't be. You're too young to have a boyfriend. You're real quiet, ain't you. I like that. I can't stand girls who yak and yak and can't shut up. I like quiet girls. You speak English? I'll teach you how to speak English.

ANON. Listen. There right there. Somebody's back there. Who's back there?

STRYGAL. Nobody.

ANON. There's people back there. I can hear them. How many people are back there?

STRYGAL. That's none of your business, pal.

ANON. It's too hot. They'll suffocate. Stop the truck.

STRYGAL. You gotta be kidding me.

ANON. I said stop the truck. Pull over.

STRYGAL. No.

> (ANON *grabs the wheel.* ANON *and* STRYGAL *struggle for control of the wheel.*)

STRYGAL. WHAT'RE YOU DOING? ARE YOU OUTTA YOUR MIND?

BELEN. STOP—

ANON. PULL OVER—

STRYGAL. NO—

BELEN. WHAT ARE YOU DOING?

ANON. I SAID PULL OVER—

STRYGAL. ARE YOU INSANE?

BELEN. WAIT—

> (*The blare of a horn. Bright light fills the cab of the truck. Crash. Darkness.*)

19.

> (*Darkness. Inside the back of Strygal's truck.* CHORUS OF REFUGEES *in the darkness.*)

CHORUS OF REFUGEES.

My name was Maria	I came to America on a ship.
My name was Ahmet	I came to America in a truck.
My name was Soo Chai	I walked a thousand miles.
My name was Roberto	I crossed a giant desert.
My name was Farid	It was so hot I couldn't breathe.
My name was Aram	It was so cold, my fingers froze.
My name was Yelena	I traveled in the night.
My name was Tiang	I always traveled in the night.
My name was Maricella	I was afraid.
My name was Sanjit	I made no sound.
My name was Pran	I was invisible.
My name was Malik	I was like the murmuring wind.
My name was Jiang tsu	I was the edge of a shadow.
My name was Fatima	I was flicker out of the corner of your eye.
My name was Yousif	I came here to make a better life.
My name was Duc	I had so many hopes.

My name was Saiid	I had so many dreams.
My name was Chia	But I died
My name was Miguel	I died
My name was Trinh	I died along the way.
My name was Faisal	Please tell my sister.
My name was Meena	Tell my brother
My name was Abraham	Tell my father
My name was Song	Tell my mother
My name was Joseph	Tell my son
My name was Alicia	Tell my daughter
Remember me	Remember me.
Remember me.	

(A howling wind. The sound of metal doors being pushed open. The CHORUS OF REFUGEES *spills out from the darkness. They are ghosts. They disperse. A howling wind.* ANON *emerges from the wreckage cut and bleeding.)*

20.

(A city. Night. The sounds of traffic. A pay phone ringing. The sounds of transistor radios playing songs from Southeast Asia and the Middle East. A fragment of a telenovela on the TV. The sound of street vendors. A distant siren. A door appears. ANON *goes through the door. He is inside a dive bar. Dim reddish light. Ancient cigarette smoke. Mirrors. A juke box plays an old song. Could be Patsy Cline. Could be something else.* SERZA *wipes down the bar. The* BARFLIES *dance.)*

SERZA. Well look at what the cat dragged in. Welcome to the last stop, stranger, the end of the road, rock bottom. Come on in. Make yourself at home. We're all friends here. The more the merrier, right?

(The BARFLIES *snort.)*

ANON. Water. Please. Can I have a glass of water?

(SERZA pours him a glass of water. ANON begins to drink.)

SERZA. I gotta charge you for that, sugar. You know that, right?

ANON. I don't have any money.

SERZA. No money? You come in here and ask me for a drink and you don't have any money? What? Does it look like I'm running some kind of charity? Is that what it looks like to you? *(To the* BAR-FLIES:) He thinks I'm running a charity.

(*The* BARFLIES *snort.* ANON *pushes the half drunk glass of water back across the bar.*)

SERZA. Never mind, take it. Just take it. It's on the house.

(ANON *drinks.* SERZA *studies him.*)

SERZA. What happened to you? You get in a fight?

ANON. No. It wasn't like that.

SERZA. What was it like?

ANON. I don't want to talk about it.

SERZA. You got someplace to go?

ANON. No.

SERZA. You're just a kid. You should go home. Just go on home.

ANON. I don't have a home. I don't have a family. I don't have that. I don't have anyone.

(ANON *starts to exit and stumbles.*)

SERZA. Hey hey hey, it's OK. It's all right.

(SERZA *cleans off the blood from the side of* ANON's *face.* ANON *lets her. The song on the juke box plays.*)

ANON. It hurts. It's like all these bad things keep happening and I can't stop them. It's like everyone I get close to, they all go away. It's like they all go away and there's nothing I can do.

(*The song on the juke box plays.*)

SERZA. Ssssh. You're getting yourself all worked up. You gotta let it go. You gotta just let it go. Dance with me. Why don't you dance with me.

(*The song on the juke box plays.* ANON *and* SERZA *begin to dance. The* BARFLIES *dance.* ANON *begins to pull away.*)

ANON. I gotta go.

SERZA. You don't want to go. Just stay. Stay a while. You can stay here as long you want. You can stay here forever.

(ANON *struggles to get out of Serza's bar. A mist rolls in. Sheets and sheets of billowing fog. The bar slowly fills with fog. The song on the juke box begins to distort.* ANON *sees* IGNACIO *walking in the distance. He pulls away from* SERZA *and approaches* IGNACIO. SERZA *recedes from view.*)

21.

(The world is engulfed in fog. The distant sound of war. IGNA-CIO is walking away. ANON tries to catch up with him, but he can't.)

ANON. Hey. Wait. Wait, come back.

(IGNACIO vanishes. STRYGAL appears. Ghostly white. He clutches the steering wheel of his truck.)

Hey. I want to talk to you. Hey.

(STRYGAL vanishes. BELEN appears. She's holding her suitcase. She's walking past ANON.)

Belen? Belen, is that you?

(BELEN turns around. ANON sees her dress is red with blood.)

Belen, wait.

(BELEN continues walking away. ANON tries to follow her, but he can't keep up. He loses her. The sound of war. PASCAL appears.)

PASCAL. Where I come from soldiers came to my village. I saw them coming, and I ran into the forest. I hid beneath the leaves. I was so still. I could hear everything. I could hear the sound of fire and men shouting. I could hear my little brother. I could hear him crying and my mother saying don't cry, don't cry. I could hear the machetes. I could hear their screams. And then it was quiet. It was so quiet. All I could hear was the sound of my heart beating. Will you remember me?

ANON. Pascal?

PASCAL. When you're old and you look back, will you remember me? Will you remember a friend who died long ago?

(PASCAL recedes from view.)

ANON. Pascal? Pascal, wait—

CHORUS OF REFUGEES.
I disappeared.
I became invisible.
I ran away.
I escaped.
I shed my skin.
I changed my name.

I became anonymous.
My name is anonymous.
My name is anonymous.
My name is anonymous.

ANON.
My name is anonymous.
My name is anonymous.
My name is anonymous.

> *(The sounds of war grow closer. The* CHORUS OF REFUGEES *disperses in all different directions. The whistling of bombs falling from the sky. They get closer.* ANON *hears a woman singing a fragment of a familiar song.* NEMASANI *becomes visible. She sings.* ANON *begins to go towards her. The sound of a bomb falling.* NAJA *appears and pulls* ANON *out of the path of the explosion. The world shatters. Brilliant light. Dust motes swirling in the light. Then darkness.)*

22.

> *(*ANON *is alone in the darkness.)*

ANON. There was a war and me and my mom, we escaped on a boat. And then there was a storm, and the boat we were on sank and lots of people drowned. I know this for a fact. And later I was in a refugee camp. And then later I was adopted by a nice American family. These are facts.

> *(Light on* NICE AMERICAN FAMILY *posing for a photograph. The* FATHER *is played by the actor playing Senator Laius, the* MOTHER *is played by the actor playing Helen Laius, and the* DAUGHTER *is played by the actor playing* CALISTA.*)*

They lived in a fancy house full of so many things. But they weren't my family and it wasn't my home. And I ran away. That's a fact, too. These are all facts. But facts are only part of the story.

> *(Camera flash. the* NICE AMERICAN FAMILY *recedes from view.)*

23.

*(Light up on RITU, ALI, and NASREEN in the kitchen of an
Indian restaurant.)*

ANON. I think that your life is made up of all these bits and pieces.
And sometimes the pieces don't fit together. There's a piece that's
missing. And you try to fill in the blanks, you try to remember, and
sometimes you can see a shape of something you can almost make
out, you can almost see a face —

RITU. Your mother's face.

ANON. Yes.

RITU. There's a place I know. On the other side of town. I worked
there when we first came to this country. I sewed clothes: blue jeans,
T shirts. It was a terrible place.

ALI. It was a sweatshop. They should've shut it down years ago.
All those women from all those different countries. So many women
from all over the world. Ah, Ritu —

RITU. Yes, Ali. Yes.

ANON. What are you saying?

RITU. It's a small world, stranger, smaller than you think.

ANON. You think my mother —? That's crazy.

RITU. Is it?

ANON. What are the chances? One in a million?

RITU. What do you have to lose? There's no way to know unless
you go and see. You've come this far. Trust me. I have an idea. Nasreen, put the rice on. Ali, get the ghee. *(To ANON:)* Now listen to me,
listen carefully.

> *(RITU explains her plan to ANON. NASREEN and ALI begin
> to prepare food. The sound of cooking. The chopping of vegetables.
> Running water. Bursts of flame. The sound of sizzling and bub-
> bling. The sound of creation. The kitchen fills with steam.)*

24.

(The kitchen transforms into the sewing factory. The SEWING LADIES sew. MR. MACKUS strides towards NEMASANI. SEWING LADY #2 follows him.)

MR. MACKUS. *(To NEMASANI:)* LIES LIES LIES! I've had it with your lies! I'm onto you. You tell me you're going to marry me when this shroud is done, but it's never going to be done, is it? Is it? Because you undo it in the night when no one's looking — except for Vanna here who happened to see what you were up to and had the decency to tell me. Thank you, Vanna. As for you, you deceitful, duplicitous, mendacious minx, your little charade is over. We're getting married now. No more stalling. No more delays.

(Enter ANON with Indian take out.)

MR. MACKUS. Who are you? What do you want? Why are you here?

ANON. Somebody ordered take out.

MR. MACKUS. Who? Not me. I didn't order any take out. I've already eaten. And they don't eat. Not when I eat. I don't know when they eat. That's not my concern. Why am I telling you this? Why am I even talking to you? I don't have to explain myself.

(NEMASANI starts to exit.)

MR. MACKUS. Where do you think you're going? We have things to do. We're getting married. And then we're going to live HAPPILY EVER AFTER! HAPPY HAPPY HAPPY! THE END!

ANON. Leave her alone.

MR. MACKUS. What did you say?

ANON. You heard me.

MR. MACKUS. Is someone talking? I think it must be a little fly is buzzing around my head. O it's not a fly. It's you. And who are you again? I'll tell you who you are. You're nobody. You're a tiny cockroach I squash with my hand. You're a piece of lint I flick off my jacket. You're chewing gum on the bottom of my shoe. You're faceless and nameless. You're a dime a dozen, people like you.

(NEMASANI tries to get free of MR. MACKUS.)

MR. MACKUS. Stop it. Be still.

NEMASANI. You're hurting me.

MR. MACKUS. Be still.

ANON. Leave her alone.

MR. MACKUS. Leave her alone. You want me to leave her alone. That's funny. You're funny. You're a funny funny guy.

> (MR. MACKUS *draws a sword.*)

MR. MACKUS. Make me, little fly.

> (NAJA *appears. She throws a sword to* ANON.)

ANON. OK. If you insist.

> (ANON *and* MR. MACKUS *battle like ancient warriors. An aerial, acrobatic battle. They twist and tumble and kick They use pieces of the sewing factory — spindles and scissors and bolts of cloth and spools of colored thread. The sound of slashing. A chaos of cloth. A tangle of thread.* ANON *corners* MR. MACKUS.)

MR. MACKUS. O please don't kill me, don't kill me, please don't kill me — what was your name, stranger? Friend? I don't think I caught it.

ANON. Call me anonymous.

> (ANON *cuts a single thread with his sword. A ton of clothes rain down from the ceiling.* MR. MACKUS *is buried in an avalanche of clothes.* NAJA *pushes open an exit door. A wind blows in from the outdoors. The sound of voices carried on the wind, echoes. the* CHORUS OF REFUGEES *echoes what came before.*)

THE CHORUS OF REFUGEES.
Where I come from is far away from here —
Is oxen in rice field —
Is hills the color of green tea —
Is jungles filled with jaguars —
And pythons thick as a grown man's thigh —
Is poison frogs the size of a thumbnail —
And squirrels that can fly from tree to tree —
Is waterfalls taller than the tallest skyscraper —
Is olive trees and ancient desert —
Is sampans and temple bells —
Is sandstorms —
And monsoon rains —
Is tapir and okapi —
And electric blue butterflies with wings as wide as my arms —

> (NEMASANI's *shroud transforms into a butterfly and flies away.*)

25.

(The rooftop of the sewing factory. Sunset. The sky is fuchsia and tangerine and indigo blue. ANON and NEMASANI are alone.)

NEMASANI. Where I come from, there are butterflies like nothing you've ever seen.

ANON. Blue.

NEMASANI. Yes, blue so blue.

ANON. With huge wings.

NEMASANI. Huge.

ANON. *(Spreading his arms:)* Like this. Bigger even.

NEMASANI. Yes. *(Recognizing something in ANON:)* Yes.

ANON. I remember.

    (NEMASANI and ANON look at each other.)

ANON. What if I told you—?

NEMASANI. No. Don't say it—

ANON. What if somehow—

NEMASANI. Please don't—

ANON. But what if—

NEMASANI. I don't believe in "what if." "What if" will break your heart.

ANON. You have a son—

NEMASANI. My son died. He died a long time ago. He was just a little boy and he died.

ANON. What if he didn't?

NEMASANI. Stop—

ANON. What if he survived?

NEMASANI. I said stop—

ANON. Please listen to me—

NEMASANI. No. No. I can't. I'm sorry. I'm so sorry.

    (NEMASANI begins to exit.)

ANON.
What do you remember?

Because what I remember, what I remember is you.
How you used to hold me.
You held me and you sang to me.
I remember the song you sang to me.

> (*Somewhere in the night the sound of a woman singing an ancient song. NEMASANI turns and looks back at ANON. She approaches him.*)

NEMASANI. How can I know you are who you say you are?

ANON.
I'll tell you the story of my life and then you can decide.
It begins in the middle
On the border
On the crossing.
It begins in the place in between.

> (*The song continues. NEMASANI approaches ANON. The sounds of the city begin to filter through and fuse with the ancient song. They make a new song. It grows like a beautiful hybrid bloom in the wilderness.*)

End of Play